T0064879

Daily Promises From God

---

365 DAYS OF ENCOURAGEMENT AND STRENGTH

BY SUSAN JONES

NEW YORK, NEW YORK

Good Books books may be purchased in bulk at special discounts for sales promotion, corporate gifts, fund-raising, or educational purposes. Special editions can also be created to specifications. For details, contact the Special Sales Department, Good Books, 307 West 36th Street, 11th Floor, New York, NY 10018 or info@skyhorsepublishing.com.

Good Books is an imprint of Skyhorse Publishing, Inc.®, a Delaware corporation.

Visit our website at www.goodbooks.com.

10 9 8 7 6 5 4 3 2

Library of Congress Cataloging-in-Publication Data is available on file.

Cover design by Michele Trombley

Print ISBN: 978-1-68099-286-1
Ebook ISBN: 978-1-68099-294-6

Printed in China

I will both lay me down in peace, and sleep: for thou, Lord, only makest me dwell in safety.

PSALMS 4:8

THIS BOOK OF THE LAW SHALL NOT DEPART OUT OF THY MOUTH; BUT THOU SHALT MEDITATE THEREIN DAY AND NIGHT, THAT THOU MAYEST OBSERVE TO DO ACCORDING TO ALL THAT IS WRITTEN THEREIN: FOR THEN THOU SHALT MAKE THY WAY PROSPEROUS, AND THEN THOU SHALT HAVE GOOD SUCCESS.

JOSHUA 1:8

MY EYES WILL WATCH OVER THEM FOR THEIR GOOD, AND I WILL BRING THEM BACK TO THIS LAND. I WILL BUILD THEM UP AND NOT TEAR THEM DOWN; I WILL PLANT THEM AND NOT UPROOT THEM.

JEREMIAH 24:6

And I will give you a new heart, and a new spirit I will put within you. And I will remove the heart of stone from your flesh and give you a heart of flesh.

EZEKIEL 36:26

ALL THAT BELONGS TO THE FATHER IS MINE . . .

JOHN 16:15

REST IN THE LORD, AND
WAIT PATIENTLY FOR
HIM: FRET NOT THYSELF
BECAUSE OF HIM WHO
PROSPERETH IN HIS WAY,
BECAUSE OF THE MAN
WHO BRINGETH WICKED
DEVICES TO PASS.

PSALMS 37:7

HOPE IN THE LORD
AND KEEP HIS WAY.
HE WILL EXALT
YOU TO INHERIT
THE LAND . . .

PSALMS 37:34

THE RIGHTEOUS WILL INHERIT THE LAND AND DWELL IN IT FOREVER.

PSALMS 37:29

THOU SHALT
KNOW ALSO
THAT THY SEED
SHALL BE GREAT,
AND THINE
OFFSPRING AS
THE GRASS OF
THE EARTH.

JOB 5:25

THE LORD TURN HIS
FACE TOWARD YOU
AND GIVE YOU PEACE.

NUMBERS 6:26

ALL YOUR CHILDREN WILL BE TAUGHT BY THE LORD, AND GREAT WILL BE THEIR PEACE.

ISAIAH 54:13

AND NOW, O LORD
GOD, THOU ART
THAT GOD, AND THY
WORDS BE TRUE,
AND THOU HAST
PROMISED THIS
GOODNESS UNTO
THY SERVANT.

2 SAMUEL 7:28

THEY SHALL
STILL BRING
FORTH FRUIT
IN OLD AGE;
THEY SHALL BE
FAT AND
FLOURISHING.

PSALMS 92:14

BUT SEEK HIS KINGDOM, AND THESE THINGS WILL BE GIVEN TO YOU AS WELL.

LUKE 12:31

THE LORD WILL MAKE YOU THE HEAD, NOT THE TAIL. IF YOU PAY ATTENTION TO THE COMMANDS OF THE LORD YOUR GOD THAT I GIVE YOU THIS DAY AND CAREFULLY FOLLOW THEM, YOU WILL ALWAYS BE AT THE TOP, NEVER AT THE BOTTOM.

DEUTERONOMY 28:13

AFFLICTED CITY,
LASHED BY STORMS
AND NOT COMFORTED,
I WILL REBUILD YOU
WITH STONES OF
TURQUOISE, YOUR
FOUNDATIONS WITH
LAPIS LAZULI.

ISAIAH 54:11

I WILL MAKE YOUR BATTLEMENTS OF RUBIES, YOUR GATES OF SPARKLING JEWELS, AND ALL YOUR WALLS OF PRECIOUS STONES.

ISAIAH 54:12

He shall deliver thee in six troubles: yea, in seven there shall no evil touch thee.

JOB 5:19

AND LET US NOT GROW WEARY OF DOING GOOD, FOR IN DUE SEASON WE WILL REAP, IF WE DO NOT GIVE UP.

GALATIANS 6:9

. . . THE PLOWMAN
SHOULD PLOW IN
HOPE, AND THE
THRESHER THRESH IN
HOPE OF SHARING IN
THE CROP.

1 CORINTHIANS 9:10

NOW TO HIM WHO
IS ABLE TO DO FAR
MORE ABUNDANTLY
THAN ALL THAT
WE ASK OR THINK,
ACCORDING TO THE
POWER AT WORK
WITHIN US . . .

EPHESIANS 3:20

Then God said, "Let us make man in our image, after our likeness. And let them have dominion over the fish of the sea and over the birds of the heavens and over the livestock and over all the earth and over every creeping thing that creeps on the earth."

I WILL BE FOUND
BY YOU, DECLARES
THE LORD, AND I
WILL RESTORE YOUR
FORTUNES AND
GATHER YOU FROM
ALL THE NATIONS
AND ALL THE PLACES
WHERE I HAVE
DRIVEN YOU . . .

JEREMIAH 29:14

MY SON, DO
NOT FORGET
MY TEACHING,
BUT LET YOUR
HEART KEEP MY
COMMANDMENTS,
FOR LENGTH OF
DAYS AND YEARS
OF LIFE AND
PEACE THEY WILL
ADD TO YOU.

PROVERBS 3:1-2

For the Lord takes pleasure in his people; he adorns the humble with salvation.

PSALMS 149:4

AND AFTER YOU HAVE
SUFFERED A LITTLE
WHILE, THE GOD OF
ALL GRACE, WHO HAS
CALLED YOU TO HIS
ETERNAL GLORY IN
CHRIST, WILL HIMSELF
RESTORE, CONFIRM,
STRENGTHEN, AND
ESTABLISH YOU.

1 PETER 5:10

AND IT SHALL COME
TO PASS, WHEN YE
BE COME TO THE
LAND WHICH THE
LORD WILL GIVE
YOU, ACCORDING AS
HE HATH PROMISED,
THAT YE SHALL
KEEP THIS SERVICE.

EXODUS 12:25

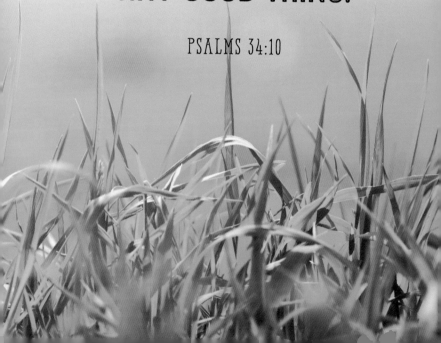

THE YOUNG LIONS
DO LACK, AND
SUFFER HUNGER:
BUT THEY THAT
SEEK THE LORD
SHALL NOT WANT
ANY GOOD THING.

PSALMS 34:10

THE LORD
REDEEMETH
THE SOUL OF
HIS SERVANTS:
AND NONE OF
THEM THAT
TRUST IN HIM
SHALL BE
DESOLATE.

PSALMS 34:22

For after all these things do the Gentiles seek: for your heavenly Father knoweth that ye have need of all these things. But seek ye first the kingdom of God, and his righteousness; and all these things shall be added unto you.

MATTHEW 6:32–33

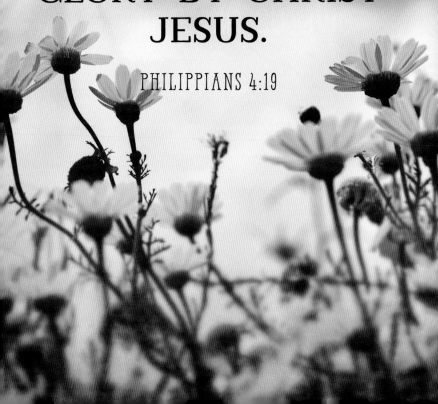

BUT MY GOD SHALL SUPPLY ALL YOUR NEED ACCORDING TO HIS RICHES IN GLORY BY CHRIST JESUS.

PHILIPPIANS 4:19

HE THAT SPARED
NOT HIS OWN SON,
BUT DELIVERED HIM
UP FOR US ALL, HOW
SHALL HE NOT WITH
HIM ALSO FREELY
GIVE US ALL THINGS?

ROMANS 8:32

THOU WILT KEEP HIM IN PERFECT PEACE, WHOSE MIND IS STAYED ON THEE: BECAUSE HE TRUSTETH IN THEE.

ISAIAH 26:3

Great peace have they which love thy law: and nothing shall offend them.

PSALMS 119:165

AT DESTRUCTION AND
FAMINE THOU SHALT
LAUGH: NEITHER SHALT
THOU BE AFRAID OF THE
BEASTS OF THE EARTH.
FOR THOU SHALT BE
IN LEAGUE WITH THE
STONES OF THE FIELD:
AND THE BEASTS OF
THE FIELD SHALL BE AT
PEACE WITH THEE.

JOB 5:22-23

PEACE I LEAVE WITH YOU, MY PEACE I GIVE UNTO YOU: NOT AS THE WORLD GIVETH, GIVE I UNTO YOU. LET NOT YOUR HEART BE TROUBLED, NEITHER LET IT BE AFRAID.

JOHN 14:27

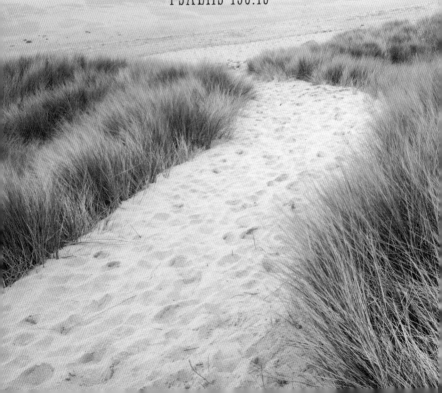

Your eyes saw my unformed body; all the days ordained for me were written in your book before one of them came to be.

PSALMS 139:16

YOUR FATHER KNOWS WHAT YOU NEED BEFORE YOU ASK HIM.

MATTHEW 6:8

Even to your old age and gray hairs I am he, I am he who will sustain you. I have made you and I will carry you; I will sustain you and, I will rescue you.

ISAIAH 46:4

LISTEN, MY DEAR BROTHERS AND SISTERS: HAS NOT GOD CHOSEN THOSE WHO ARE POOR IN THE EYES OF THE WORLD TO BE RICH IN FAITH AND TO INHERIT THE KINGDOM HE PROMISED THOSE WHO LOVE HIM?

JAMES 2:5

THE BLAMELESS SPEND THEIR DAYS UNDER THE LORD'S CARE, AND THEIR INHERITANCE WILL ENDURE FOREVER.

PSALMS 37:18

LET US THEN
APPROACH GOD'S
THRONE OF GRACE
WITH CONFIDENCE, SO
THAT WE MAY RECEIVE
MERCY AND FIND
GRACE TO HELP US IN
OUR TIME OF NEED.

HEBREWS 4:16

Yet the Lord longs
to be gracious
to you; therefore
he will rise up
to show you
compassion. For
the Lord is a God
of justice . . .

ISAIAH 30:18

YOU NEED TO PERSEVERE SO THAT WHEN YOU HAVE DONE THE WILL OF GOD, YOU WILL RECEIVE WHAT HE HAS PROMISED.

HEBREWS 10:36

WE DO NOT WANT YOU TO BECOME LAZY, BUT TO IMITATE THOSE WHO, THROUGH FAITH AND PATIENCE, INHERIT WHAT HAS BEEN PROMISED.

HEBREWS 6:12

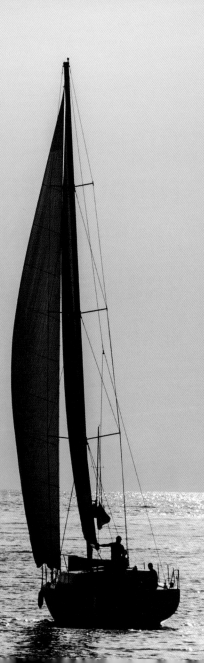

YOU ARE
WORTHY, OUR
LORD AND GOD,
TO RECEIVE
GLORY AND
HONOR AND
POWER, FOR YOU
CREATED ALL
THINGS, AND BY
YOUR WILL THEY
EXISTED AND
WERE CREATED.

REVELATION 4:11

Every generous act of giving, with every perfect gift, is from above, coming down from the Father of lights, with whom there is no variation or shadow due to change.

JAMES 1:17

HE COVERS
THE HEAVENS
WITH CLOUDS,
PREPARES
RAIN FOR THE
EARTH, MAKES
GRASS GROW
ON THE HILLS.

PSALMS 147:8

TO DO
RIGHTEOUSNESS AND
JUSTICE IS MORE
ACCEPTABLE TO THE
LORD THAN SACRIFICE.

PROVERBS 21:3

I will put my Spirit within you, and you shall live, and I will place you on your own soil; then you shall know that I, the Lord, have spoken and will act, says the Lord.

EZEKIEL 37:14

[THE LORD]
WHO EXECUTES
JUSTICE
FOR THE
OPPRESSED;
WHO GIVES
FOOD TO THE
HUNGRY . . .

PSALMS 146:7

. . . THE GOD OF ALL GRACE, WHO HAS CALLED YOU TO HIS ETERNAL GLORY IN CHRIST, WILL HIMSELF RESTORE, SUPPORT, STRENGTHEN, AND ESTABLISH YOU.

1 PETER 5:10

FOR AS THE RAIN AND THE SNOW
COME DOWN FROM HEAVEN, AND
DO NOT RETURN THERE UNTIL
THEY HAVE WATERED THE EARTH,
MAKING IT BRING FORTH AND
SPROUT, GIVING SEED TO THE
SOWER AND BREAD TO THE EATER.

ISAIAH 55:10

YOU OPEN
YOUR HAND,
SATISFYING THE
DESIRE OF EVERY
LIVING THING.

PSALMS 145:16

God said, "See, I have given you every plant yielding seed that is upon the face of all the earth, and every tree with seed in its fruit; you shall have them for food."

GENESIS 1:29

I WILL MAKE THE FRUIT OF THE TREE AND THE PRODUCE OF THE FIELD ABUNDANT, SO THAT YOU MAY NEVER AGAIN SUFFER THE DISGRACE OF FAMINE AMONG THE NATIONS.

EZEKIEL 36:30

. . . HE STANDS
AT THE RIGHT
HAND OF THE
NEEDY . . .

PSALMS 109:31

FOR HE SATISFIES THE LONGING SOUL, AND THE HUNGRY SOUL HE FILLS WITH GOOD THINGS.

PSALMS 107:9

AND I BROUGHT YOU
INTO A PLENTIFUL
LAND TO ENJOY ITS
FRUITS AND ITS
GOOD THINGS.

JEREMIAH 2:7

Whoever brings blessing will be enriched, and one who waters will himself be watered.

PROVERBS 11:25

THE LAMBS WILL PROVIDE YOUR CLOTHING, AND THE GOATS THE PRICE OF A FIELD. THERE WILL BE ENOUGH GOATS' MILK FOR YOUR FOOD, FOR THE FOOD OF YOUR HOUSEHOLD . . .

PROVERBS 27:26–27

GOD SETTLES THE SOLITARY IN A HOME . . .

PSALMS 68:6

TO THE LORD
OUR GOD BELONG
MERCIES AND
FORGIVENESSES,
THOUGH WE
HAVE REBELLED
AGAINST HIM . . .

DANIEL 9:9

. . . CHRIST
HAS SET
US FREE. . . .

GALATIANS 5:1

In whom we have redemption through his blood, even the forgiveness of sins . . .

COLOSSIANS 1:14

[THE LORD] WHO
FORGIVETH ALL
THINE INIQUITIES;
WHO HEALETH ALL
THY DISEASES . . .

PSALMS 103:3

[THE LORD] WHO
REDEEMETH THY LIFE
FROM DESTRUCTION; WHO
CROWNETH THEE WITH
LOVING KINDNESS AND
TENDER MERCIES . . .

PSALMS 103:4

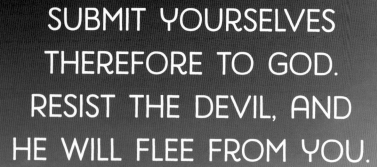

SUBMIT YOURSELVES
THEREFORE TO GOD.
RESIST THE DEVIL, AND
HE WILL FLEE FROM YOU.

JAMES 4:7

Draw nigh to God, and he will draw nigh to you. Cleanse your hands, ye sinners; and purify your hearts, ye double minded.

JAMES 4:8

For in that he himself hath suffered being tempted, he is able to succour them that are tempted.

HEBREWS 2:18

BEHOLD, HAPPY IS
THE MAN WHOM
GOD CORRECTETH:
THEREFORE DESPISE
NOT THOU THE
CHASTENING OF
THE ALMIGHTY.

JOB 5:17

BUT IF WE WALK IN THE LIGHT, AS HE IS IN THE LIGHT, WE HAVE FELLOWSHIP ONE WITH ANOTHER, AND THE BLOOD OF JESUS CHRIST, HIS SON, CLEANSETH US FROM ALL SIN.

1 JOHN 1:7

THE LORD HELPS THEM
AND DELIVERS THEM;
HE DELIVERS THEM
FROM THE WICKED
AND SAVES THEM,
BECAUSE THEY TAKE
REFUGE IN HIM.

PSALMS 37:40

Because the Lord your God is a merciful God, he will neither abandon you nor destroy you; he will not forget the covenant with your ancestors that he swore to them.

DEUTERONOMY 4:31

. . . HE DOES NOT
RETAIN HIS ANGER
FOREVER, BECAUSE
HE DELIGHTS IN
SHOWING CLEMENCY.

MICAH 7:18

AND ALL WHO HAVE THIS HOPE IN HIM PURIFY THEMSELVES, JUST AS HE IS PURE.

1 JOHN 3:3

In Christ God was reconciling the world to himself, not counting their trespasses against them, and entrusting the message of reconciliation to us.

2 CORINTHIANS 5:19

AS FAR AS THE
EAST IS FROM
THE WEST, SO FAR
HE REMOVES OUR
TRANSGRESSIONS
FROM US.

PSALMS 103:12

In him you also, when you had heard the word of truth, the gospel of your salvation, and had believed in him, were marked with the seal of the promised Holy Spirit . . .

EPHESIANS 1:13

I HAVE SWEPT AWAY YOUR TRANSGRESSIONS LIKE A CLOUD, AND YOUR SINS LIKE MIST; RETURN TO ME, FOR I HAVE REDEEMED YOU.

ISAIAH 44:22

FOR YOU ARE A PEOPLE HOLY TO THE LORD YOUR GOD. THE LORD YOUR GOD HAS CHOSEN YOU TO BE A PEOPLE FOR HIS TREASURED POSSESSION, OUT OF ALL THE PEOPLES WHO ARE ON THE FACE OF THE EARTH.

DEUTERONOMY 7:6

LOVE DOES NOT DELIGHT IN EVIL BUT REJOICES WITH THE TRUTH. IT ALWAYS PROTECTS, ALWAYS TRUSTS, ALWAYS HOPES, ALWAYS PERSEVERES.

1 CORINTHIANS 13:6-7

RIGHTEOUSNESS
AND JUSTICE ARE
THE FOUNDATION OF
YOUR THRONE; LOVE
AND FAITHFULNESS
GO BEFORE YOU.

PSALMS 89:14

Be afflicted, and mourn, and weep: let your laughter be turned to mourning, and your joy to heaviness.

JAMES 4:9

HUMBLE
YOURSELVES
IN THE SIGHT
OF THE
LORD, AND
HE SHALL
LIFT YOU UP.

JAMES 4:10

Let what you heard from the beginning abide in you. If what you heard from the beginning abides in you, then you will abide in the Son and in the Father.

1 JOHN 2:24

FOR THE LORD
WILL NOT FORSAKE
HIS PEOPLE, FOR
HIS GREAT NAME'S
SAKE, BECAUSE IT
HAS PLEASED THE
LORD TO MAKE
YOU A PEOPLE
FOR HIMSELF.

1 SAMUEL 12:22

WHEN YOU SEARCH FOR ME, YOU WILL FIND ME; IF YOU SEEK ME WITH ALL YOUR HEART . . .

JEREMIAH 29:13

FOR HE WHO SANCTIFIES AND THOSE WHO ARE SANCTIFIED ALL HAVE ONE SOURCE. THAT IS WHY HE IS NOT ASHAMED TO CALL THEM BROTHERS . . .

HEBREWS 2:11

I WILL PUT MY LAW
WITHIN THEM, AND
I WILL WRITE IT ON
THEIR HEARTS. AND
I WILL BE THEIR GOD,
AND THEY SHALL BE
MY PEOPLE.

JEREMIAH 31:33

Love has been perfected among us in this: that we may have boldness on the day of judgment, because as he is, so are we in this world.

1 JOHN 4:17

Beloved, we are God's children now, and what we will be has not yet appeared; but we know that when he appears we shall be like him, because we shall see him as he is.

1 JOHN 3:2

YOU SHALL DWELL IN THE LAND THAT I GAVE TO YOUR FATHERS, AND YOU SHALL BE MY PEOPLE, AND I WILL BE YOUR GOD.

EZEKIEL 36:28

"THE FATHER
AND I ARE ONE."

JOHN 10:30

BUT I SAY TO YOU, LOVE YOUR ENEMIES AND PRAY FOR THOSE WHO PERSECUTE YOU, SO THAT YOU MAY BE SONS OF YOUR FATHER WHO IS IN HEAVEN.

MATTHEW 5:44-45

. . . HE WHO IS BOTH THEIR MASTER AND YOURS IS IN HEAVEN, AND THERE IS NO FAVORITISM WITH HIM.

EPHESIANS 6:9

NO, THE FATHER
HIMSELF LOVES YOU
BECAUSE YOU HAVE
LOVED ME AND HAVE
BELIEVED THAT I CAME
FROM GOD.

JOHN 16:27

WHEN THOU
PASSEST THROUGH
THE WATERS, I WILL
BE WITH THEE . . .

ISAIAH 43:2

SURELY YOUR
GOODNESS
AND LOVE WILL
FOLLOW ME ALL
THE DAYS OF
MY LIFE . . .

PSALMS 23:6

. . . God our Father . . .
loved us and by his
grace gave us eternal
encouragement and
good hope . . .

2 THESSALONIANS 2:16

NOW, IF WE ARE CHILDREN, THEN WE ARE HEIRS—HEIRS OF GOD AND CO-HEIRS WITH CHRIST, IF INDEED WE SHARE IN HIS SUFFERINGS IN ORDER THAT WE MAY ALSO SHARE IN HIS GLORY.

ROMANS 8:17

THE SPIRIT HIMSELF TESTIFIES WITH OUR SPIRIT THAT WE ARE GOD'S CHILDREN.

ROMANS 8:16

. . . THE SPIRIT YOU RECEIVED BROUGHT ABOUT YOUR ADOPTION TO SONSHIP. AND BY HIM WE CRY, "ABBA, FATHER."

ROMANS 8:15

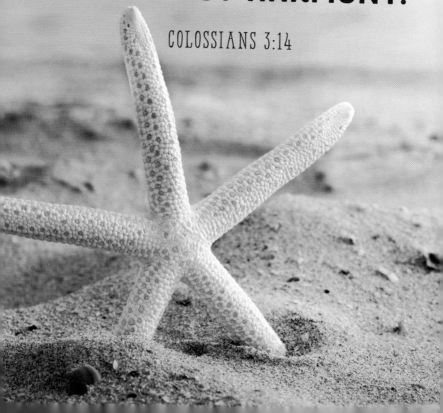

ABOVE ALL, CLOTHE YOURSELVES WITH LOVE, WHICH BINDS EVERYTHING TOGETHER IN PERFECT HARMONY.

COLOSSIANS 3:14

AND NOW FAITH, HOPE, AND LOVE ABIDE, THESE THREE; AND THE GREATEST OF THESE IS LOVE.

1 CORINTHIANS 13:13

JUST AS
WATER
REFLECTS
THE FACE, SO
ONE HUMAN
HEART
REFLECTS
ANOTHER.

PROVERBS 27:19

He destined us for adoption as his children through Jesus Christ, according to the good pleasure of his will . . .

EPHESIANS 1:5

FOR THE LORD IS GOOD; HIS STEADFAST LOVE ENDURES FOREVER, AND HIS FAITHFULNESS TO ALL GENERATIONS.

PSALMS 100:5

HOW PRECIOUS IS
YOUR STEADFAST
LOVE, O GOD!
ALL PEOPLE MAY
TAKE REFUGE IN
THE SHADOW OF
YOUR WINGS.

PSALMS 36:7

THE LORD
APPEARED TO
HIM FROM FAR
AWAY. I HAVE
LOVED YOU WITH
AN EVERLASTING
LOVE; THEREFORE,
I HAVE CONTINUED
MY FAITHFULNESS
TO YOU.

JEREMIAH 31:3

And hope does not disappoint us, because God's love has been poured into our hearts through the Holy Spirit that has been given to us.

ROMANS 5:5

THE STEADFAST LOVE OF THE LORD NEVER CEASES, HIS MERCIES NEVER COME TO AN END.

LAMENTATIONS 3:22

. . . CHRIST MAY DWELL IN YOUR HEARTS THROUGH FAITH, AS YOU ARE BEING ROOTED AND GROUNDED IN LOVE.

EPHESIANS 3:17

YOUR STEADFAST LOVE, O LORD, EXTENDS TO THE HEAVENS, YOUR FAITHFULNESS TO THE CLOUDS.

PSALMS 36:5

For the Lord reproves the one he loves, as a father the son in whom he delights.

PROVERBS 3:12

FOR THE MOUNTAINS MAY DEPART AND THE HILLS BE REMOVED, BUT MY STEADFAST LOVE SHALL NOT DEPART FROM YOU . . .

ISAIAH 54:10

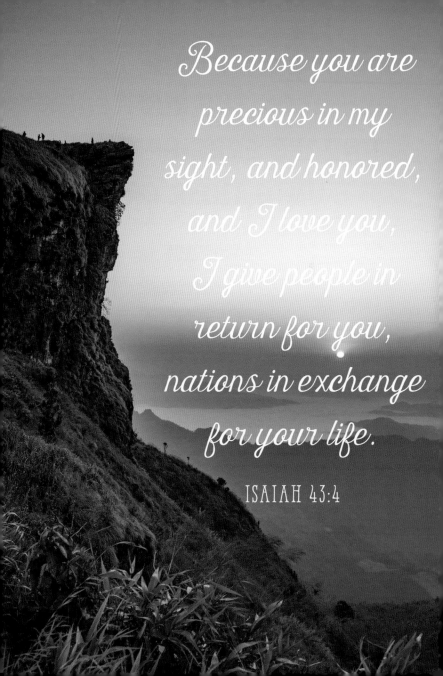

Because you are precious in my sight, and honored, and I love you, I give people in return for you, nations in exchange for your life.

ISAIAH 43:4

THE EYES OF THE LORD
ARE UPON THE RIGHTEOUS,
AND HIS EARS ARE OPEN
UNTO THEIR CRY.

PSALMS 34:15

AND THE PEACE
OF GOD, WHICH
PASSETH ALL
UNDERSTANDING,
SHALL KEEP YOUR
HEARTS AND
MINDS THROUGH
CHRIST JESUS.

PHILIPPIANS 4:7

I WILL REJOICE AND
BE GLAD IN YOUR
STEADFAST LOVE,
BECAUSE YOU HAVE
SEEN MY AFFLICTION . . .

PSALMS 31:7

HAVE NOT I COMMANDED THEE? BE STRONG AND OF A GOOD COURAGE; BE NOT AFRAID, NEITHER BE THOU DISMAYED: FOR THE LORD THY GOD IS WITH THEE WHITHERSOEVER THOU GOEST.

JOSHUA 1:9

THE SPIRIT OF THE LORD GOD IS UPON ME . . .

ISAIAH 61:1

I WAITED PATIENTLY FOR THE LORD; HE TURNED TO ME AND HEARD MY CRY.

PSALMS 40:1

YOU KNOW
WHEN I SIT
AND WHEN
I RISE; YOU
PERCEIVE MY
THOUGHTS
FROM AFAR.

PSALMS 139:2

IF WE ARE FAITHLESS, HE REMAINS FAITHFUL . . .

2 TIMOTHY 2:13

You discern my going out and my lying down; you are familiar with all my ways.

PSALMS 139:3

IF I GO UP TO THE
HEAVENS, YOU ARE
THERE; IF I MAKE MY
BED IN THE DEPTHS,
YOU ARE THERE.

PSALMS 139:8

"BE STRONG AND COURAGEOUS. DO NOT BE AFRAID OR TERRIFIED BECAUSE OF THEM, FOR THE LORD YOUR GOD GOES WITH YOU; HE WILL NEVER LEAVE YOU NOR FORSAKE YOU."

DEUTERONOMY 31:6

The grace of the Lord Jesus Christ
be with your spirit. Amen.

PHILIPPIANS 4:23

. . . CASTING ALL YOUR ANXIETIES ON HIM, BECAUSE HE CARES FOR YOU.

1 PETER 5:7

Call to me and I will answer you, and will tell you great and hidden things that you have not known.

JEREMIAH 33:3

. . . HOW MUCH MORE WILL YOUR FATHER WHO IS IN HEAVEN GIVE GOOD THINGS TO THOSE WHO ASK HIM!

MATTHEW 7:11

ASK, AND
IT WILL BE
GIVEN TO
YOU; SEEK,
AND YOU WILL
FIND; KNOCK,
AND IT WILL
BE OPENED
TO YOU.

MATTHEW 7:7

THEN YOU WILL CALL UPON ME AND COME AND PRAY TO ME, AND I WILL HEAR YOU.

JEREMIAH 29:12

AND THIS IS THE
CONFIDENCE
THAT WE HAVE
TOWARD HIM,
THAT IF WE
ASK ANYTHING
ACCORDING TO
HIS WILL HE
HEARS US.

1 JOHN 5:14

YOU MEET HIM WHO
JOYFULLY WORKS
RIGHTEOUSNESS, THOSE
WHO REMEMBER YOU
IN YOUR WAYS.

ISAIAH 64:5

FOR WHERE TWO
OR THREE ARE
GATHERED IN MY
NAME, THERE AM I
AMONG THEM.

MATTHEW 18:20

He will not let your foot be moved; he who keeps you will not slumber.

PSALMS 121:3

. . . FROM
WHERE HE SITS
ENTHRONED
HE LOOKS OUT
ON ALL THE
INHABITANTS OF
THE EARTH . . .

PSALMS 33:14

. . . FOR IT IS GOD WHO WORKS IN YOU, BOTH TO WILL AND TO WORK FOR HIS GOOD PLEASURE.

PHILIPPIANS 2:13

The Lord watches
over the sojourners;
he upholds the widow
and the fatherless . . .

PSALMS 146:9

AND THOSE
WHO KNOW
YOUR NAME PUT
THEIR TRUST IN
YOU, FOR YOU,
O LORD, HAVE
NOT FORSAKEN
THOSE WHO
SEEK YOU.

PSALMS 9:10

*The grace
of our Lord
Jesus Christ be
with you.*

1 THESSALONIANS 5:28

KEEP YOUR LIFE
FREE FROM LOVE
OF MONEY, AND BE
CONTENT WITH WHAT
YOU HAVE, FOR HE
HAS SAID, "I WILL
NEVER LEAVE YOU
NOR FORSAKE YOU."

HEBREWS 13:5

BUT THE STEADFAST LOVE OF THE LORD IS FROM EVERLASTING TO EVERLASTING . . .

PSALMS 103:17

THE RIGHTEOUS CRY, AND THE LORD HEARETH, AND DELIVERETH THEM OUT OF ALL THEIR TROUBLES.

PSALMS 34:17

IN FAMINE HE
SHALL REDEEM
THEE FROM DEATH:
AND IN WAR,
FROM THE POWER
OF THE SWORD.

JOB 5:20

FOR THE LORD GOD IS A SUN AND SHIELD: THE LORD WILL GIVE GRACE AND GLORY: NO GOOD THING WILL HE WITHHOLD FROM THEM THAT WALK UPRIGHTLY.

PSALMS 84:11

. . . NO WEAPON THAT IS FASHIONED AGAINST YOU SHALL SUCCEED, AND YOU SHALL REFUTE EVERY TONGUE THAT RISES AGAINST YOU IN JUDGMENT. THIS IS THE HERITAGE OF THE SERVANTS OF THE LORD . . .

ISAIAH 54:17

I sought the Lord, and he heard me, and delivered me from all my fears.

PSALMS 34:4

WE KNOW THAT
WHOSOEVER IS BORN
OF GOD SINNETH
NOT; BUT HE THAT
IS BEGOTTEN OF GOD
KEEPETH HIMSELF,
AND THAT WICKED ONE
TOUCHETH HIM NOT.

1 JOHN 5:18

HE TOOK UP
OUR INFIRMITIES
AND BORE OUR
DISEASES.

MATTHEW 8:17

THE NAME OF THE LORD IS A STRONG TOWER: THE RIGHTEOUS RUNNETH INTO IT, AND IS SAFE.

PROVERBS 18:10

Though I walk in
the midst of trouble,
thou wilt revive me:
thou shalt stretch
forth thine hand
against the wrath of
mine enemies, and
thy right hand shall
save me.

PSALMS 138:7

As one whom
his mother
comforteth,
so will I
comfort you;
and ye shall be
comforted in
Jerusalem.

ISAIAH 66:13

THOU SHALT BE HID
FROM THE SCOURGE OF
THE TONGUE: NEITHER
SHALT THOU BE AFRAID
OF DESTRUCTION WHEN
IT COMETH.

JOB 5:21

FOR I WILL RESTORE
HEALTH UNTO
THEE, AND I WILL
HEAL THEE OF THY
WOUNDS, SAITH
THE LORD; BECAUSE
THEY CALLED
THEE AN OUTCAST,
SAYING, THIS IS
ZION, WHOM NO MAN
SEEKETH AFTER.

JEREMIAH 30:17

And said, "If thou wilt diligently hearken to the voice of the Lord thy God, and wilt do that which is right in his sight, and wilt give ear to his commandments, and keep all his statutes, I will put none of these diseases upon thee . . . for I am the Lord that healeth thee."

EXODUS 15:26

[THE LORD] WHO SATISFIETH THY MOUTH WITH GOOD THINGS; SO THAT THY YOUTH IS RENEWED LIKE THE EAGLE'S.

PSALMS 103:5

BUT THUS SAITH THE LORD, EVEN THE CAPTIVES OF THE MIGHTY SHALL BE TAKEN AWAY, AND THE PREY OF THE TERRIBLE SHALL BE DELIVERED: FOR I WILL CONTEND WITH HIM THAT CONTENDETH WITH THEE, AND I WILL SAVE THY CHILDREN.

ISAIAH 49:25

IF YE . . . KNOW HOW TO GIVE GOOD GIFTS UNTO YOUR CHILDREN: HOW MUCH MORE SHALL YOUR HEAVENLY FATHER GIVE THE HOLY SPIRIT TO THEM THAT ASK HIM?

LUKE 11:13

EVEN THOUGH I
WALK THROUGH
THE DARKEST
VALLEY, I WILL
FEAR NO EVIL, FOR
YOU ARE WITH ME;
YOUR ROD AND
YOUR STAFF, THEY
COMFORT ME.

PSALMS 23:4

No harm will overtake you, no disaster will come near your tent.

PSALMS 91:10

LET THE BELOVED
OF THE LORD REST
SECURE IN HIM,
FOR HE SHIELDS
HIM ALL DAY
LONG, AND THE
ONE THE LORD
LOVES RESTS
BETWEEN HIS
SHOULDERS.

DEUTERONOMY 33:12

YOU PROVIDE A
BROAD PATH FOR
MY FEET, SO THAT
MY ANKLES DO
NOT GIVE WAY.

2 SAMUEL 22:37

For in the day of
trouble he will
keep me safe in
his dwelling; he
will hide me in the
shelter of his sacred
tent and set me high
upon a rock.

PSALMS 27:5

EVEN THE DARKNESS
WILL NOT BE DARK
TO YOU; THE NIGHT
WILL SHINE LIKE THE
DAY, FOR DARKNESS
IS AS LIGHT TO YOU.

PSALMS 139:12

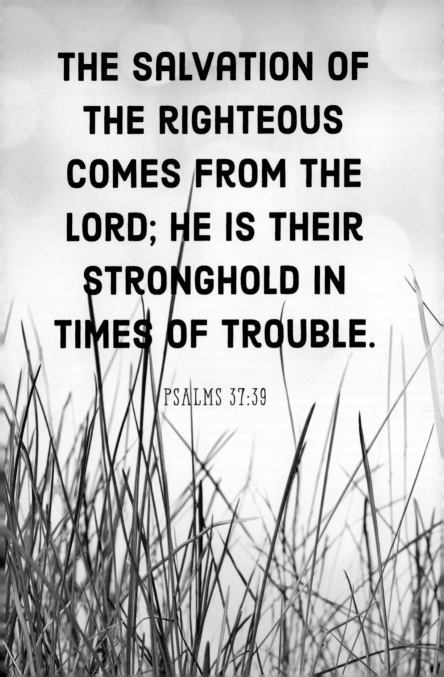

IN TIMES OF DISASTER
THEY WILL NOT
WITHER; IN DAYS OF
FAMINE THEY WILL
ENJOY PLENTY.

PSALMS 37:19

He makes wars cease to the ends of the earth . . .

PSALMS 46:9

THE LORD ALMIGHTY IS WITH US; THE GOD OF JACOB IS OUR FORTRESS.

PSALMS 46:11

YOU, LORD, WILL
KEEP THE NEEDY
SAFE AND WILL
PROTECT US
FOREVER FROM
THE WICKED . . .

PSALMS 12:7

IN RIGHTEOUSNESS YOU WILL BE ESTABLISHED: TYRANNY WILL BE FAR FROM YOU; YOU WILL HAVE NOTHING TO FEAR. TERROR WILL BE FAR REMOVED; IT WILL NOT COME NEAR YOU.

ISAIAH 54:14

IF ANYONE DOES ATTACK YOU, IT WILL NOT BE MY DOING; WHOEVER ATTACKS YOU, WILL SURRENDER TO YOU.

ISAIAH 54:15

The Lord will grant that the enemies who rise up against you will be defeated before you. They will come at you from one direction, but flee from you in seven.

DEUTERONOMY 28:7

ONE OF YOU ROUTS A THOUSAND, BECAUSE THE LORD YOUR GOD FIGHTS FOR YOU, JUST AS HE PROMISED.

JOSHUA 23:10

. . . THE LORD KNOWS HOW TO RESCUE THE GODLY FROM TRIALS . . .

2 PETER 2:9

MY EYES ARE
EVER TOWARD
THE LORD, FOR
HE WILL PLUCK
MY FEET OUT
OF THE NET.

PSALMS 25:15

All my bones shall say,
"O Lord, who is like
you, delivering the
poor from him who is
too strong for him"...

PSALMS 35:10

THEREFORE, BROTHERS,
BE ALL THE MORE
DILIGENT TO CONFIRM
YOUR CALLING AND
ELECTION, FOR IF
YOU PRACTICE THESE
QUALITIES YOU WILL
NEVER FALL.

2 PETER 1:10

THE LORD PRESERVES THE SIMPLE; WHEN I WAS BROUGHT LOW, HE SAVED ME.

PSALMS 116:6

For you have delivered my soul from death, my eyes from tears, my feet from stumbling . . .

PSALMS 116:8

FATHER
OF THE
FATHERLESS
AND
PROTECTOR
OF WIDOWS
IS GOD IN
HIS HOLY
HABITATION.

PSALMS 68:5

Then shall your light break forth like the dawn, and your healing shall spring up speedily; your righteousness shall go before you; the glory of the Lord shall be your rear guard.

ISAIAH 58:8

GOD, THE LORD, IS MY STRENGTH; HE MAKES MY FEET LIKE THE DEER'S; HE MAKES ME TREAD ON MY HIGH PLACES.

HABAKKUK 3:19

. . . DO NOT BE GRIEVED, FOR THE JOY OF THE LORD IS YOUR STRENGTH.

NEHEMIAH 8:10

THE LORD
IS GOOD, A
STRONGHOLD
IN THE DAY
OF TROUBLE;
HE KNOWS
THOSE WHO
TAKE REFUGE
IN HIM.

NAHUM 1:7

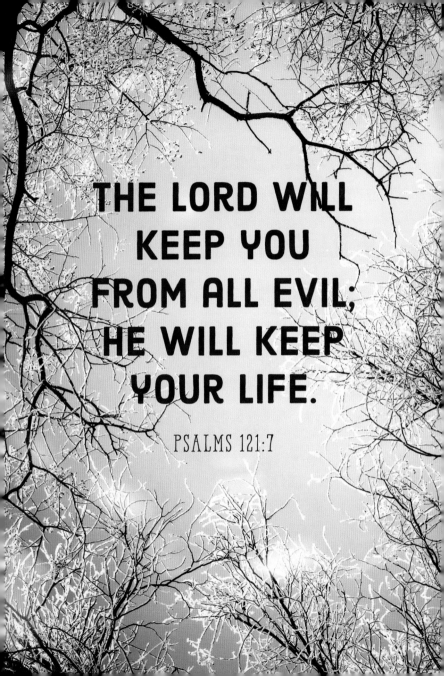

THE LORD WILL KEEP YOU FROM ALL EVIL; HE WILL KEEP YOUR LIFE.

PSALMS 121:7

HE WILL TEND HIS FLOCK
LIKE A SHEPHERD; HE
WILL GATHER THE LAMBS
IN HIS ARMS; HE WILL
CARRY THEM IN HIS
BOSOM, AND GENTLY
LEAD THOSE THAT ARE
WITH YOUNG.

ISAIAH 40:11

He alone is my rock and my salvation, my fortress; I shall not be greatly shaken.

PSALMS 62:2

THE LORD
YOUR GOD
WHO GOES
BEFORE
YOU WILL
HIMSELF
FIGHT FOR
YOU . . .

DEUTERONOMY 1:30

HE PRESERVES THE LIVES OF HIS SAINTS . . .

PSALMS 97:10

Blessed be
the Lord, who
daily bears
us up; God is
our salvation.

PSALMS 68:19

WHEN YOU PASS
THROUGH THE WATERS,
I WILL BE WITH YOU;
AND THROUGH THE
RIVERS, THEY SHALL
NOT OVERWHELM YOU;
WHEN YOU WALK
THROUGH FIRE YOU
SHALL NOT BE BURNED,
AND THE FLAME SHALL
NOT CONSUME YOU.

ISAIAH 43:2

WHEN THE CARES OF MY HEART ARE MANY, YOUR CONSOLATIONS CHEER MY SOUL.

PSALMS 94:19

A THOUSAND MAY
FALL AT YOUR SIDE,
TEN THOUSAND AT
YOUR RIGHT HAND,
BUT IT WILL NOT
COME NEAR YOU.

PSALMS 91:7

The Lord is near to the brokenhearted, and saves the crushed in spirit.

PSALMS 34:18

IN THE FEAR OF THE LORD ONE HAS STRONG CONFIDENCE, AND HIS CHILDREN WILL HAVE A REFUGE.

PROVERBS 14:26

... WE GROAN, BEING
BURDENED—NOT THAT WE
WOULD BE UNCLOTHED, BUT
THAT WE WOULD BE FURTHER
CLOTHED, SO THAT WHAT IS
MORTAL MAY BE SWALLOWED UP
BY LIFE. HE WHO HAS PREPARED
US FOR THIS VERY THING IS GOD,
WHO HAS GIVEN US THE SPIRIT
AS A GUARANTEE.

2 CORINTHIANS 5:4–5

THE LORD, GOD OF
YOUR FATHERS, MAKE
YOU A THOUSAND
TIMES SO MANY MORE
AS YE ARE, AND BLESS
YOU, AS HE HATH
PROMISED YOU!

DEUTERONOMY 1:11

BLESSED ARE THE
PEACEMAKERS:
FOR THEY SHALL
BE CALLED THE
CHILDREN OF GOD.

MATTHEW 5:9

BLESSED IS THE MAN THAT ENDURETH TEMPTATION: FOR WHEN HE IS TRIED, HE SHALL RECEIVE THE CROWN OF LIFE, WHICH THE LORD HATH PROMISED TO THEM THAT LOVE HIM.

JAMES 1:12

BLESSED ARE THE POOR IN SPIRIT: FOR THEIRS IS THE KINGDOM OF HEAVEN.

MATTHEW 5:3

FOR BY GRACE YOU HAVE BEEN SAVED THROUGH FAITH, AND THIS IS NOT YOUR OWN DOING; IT IS THE GIFT OF GOD . . .

EPHESIANS 2:8

BLESSED
ARE THEY
THAT
MOURN:
FOR THEY
SHALL BE
COMFORTED.

MATTHEW 5:4

BLESSED
ARE THE
MEEK: FOR
THEY SHALL
INHERIT THE
EARTH.

MATTHEW 5:5

BLESSED ARE
THEY WHICH DO
HUNGER AND
THIRST AFTER
RIGHTEOUSNESS:
FOR THEY SHALL
BE FILLED.

MATTHEW 5:6

Blessed are the merciful: for they shall obtain mercy.

MATTHEW 5:7

NOW THE
LORD IS THE
SPIRIT, AND
WHERE THE
SPIRIT OF
THE LORD
IS, THERE IS
FREEDOM.

2 CORINTHIANS 3:17

BLESSED ARE THE PURE IN HEART: FOR THEY SHALL SEE GOD.

MATTHEW 5:8

BLESSED ARE THE PEACEMAKERS: FOR THEY SHALL BE CALLED THE CHILDREN OF GOD.

MATTHEW 5:9

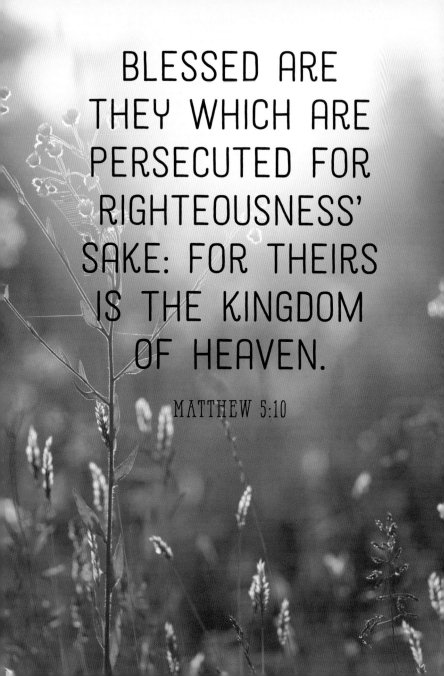

Blessed are ye, when men shall revile you, and persecute you, and shall say all manner of evil against you falsely, for my sake.

MATTHEW 5:11

Blessed is the one who does not walk in step with the wicked or stand in the way that sinners take or sit in the company of mockers, but whose delight is in the law of the Lord, and who meditates on his law day and night.

PSALMS 1:1–2

THE LORD MAKE
HIS FACE SHINE
ON YOU AND BE
GRACIOUS TO YOU.

NUMBERS 6:25

THEY ARE ALWAYS
GENEROUS AND
LEND FREELY; THEIR
CHILDREN WILL BE A
BLESSING.

PSALMS 37:26

BLESSED ARE
THOSE WHOSE
WAYS ARE
BLAMELESS,
WHO WALK
ACCORDING TO
THE LAW OF
THE LORD.

PSALMS 119:1

SURELY, LORD,
YOU BLESS THE
RIGHTEOUS; YOU
SURROUND THEM
WITH YOUR
FAVOR AS WITH
A SHIELD.

PSALMS 5:12

The Lord will open the heavens, the storehouse of his bounty, to send rain on your land in season and to bless all the work of your hands . . .

DEUTERONOMY 28:12

THE LORD WILL SEND A BLESSING ON YOUR BARNS, AND ON EVERYTHING YOU PUT YOUR HAND TO. THE LORD YOUR GOD WILL BLESS YOU IN THE LAND HE IS GIVING YOU.

DEUTERONOMY 28:8

THE FRUIT OF YOUR
WOMB WILL BE
BLESSED, AND THE
CROPS OF YOUR LAND
AND THE YOUNG OF
YOUR LIVESTOCK—THE
CALVES OF YOUR HERDS
AND THE LAMBS OF
YOUR FLOCKS.

DEUTERONOMY 28:4

YOU WILL BE BLESSED IN THE CITY AND BLESSED IN THE COUNTRY.

DEUTERONOMY 28:3

YOUR BASKET
AND YOUR
KNEADING
TROUGH WILL
BE BLESSED.

DEUTERONOMY 28:5

YOU WILL BE
BLESSED WHEN
YOU COME IN AND
BLESSED WHEN
YOU GO OUT.

DEUTERONOMY 28:6

Taste and see that the Lord is good; blessed is the one who takes refuge in him.

PSALMS 34:8

FOR I WILL POUR
WATER ON THE
THIRSTY LAND,
AND STREAMS
ON THE DRY
GROUND; I WILL
POUR OUT MY
SPIRIT ON YOUR
OFFSPRING, AND
MY BLESSING
ON YOUR
DESCENDANTS.

ISAIAH 44:3

YOU SHALL EAT THE FRUIT OF THE LABOR OF YOUR HANDS; YOU SHALL BE BLESSED, AND IT SHALL BE WELL WITH YOU.

PSALMS 128:2

Then the King will say to those on his right, "Come, you who are blessed by my Father, inherit the kingdom prepared for you from the foundation of the world."

MATTHEW 25:34

AND ALL THESE
BLESSINGS
SHALL COME
UPON YOU AND
OVERTAKE YOU,
IF YOU OBEY
THE VOICE OF
THE LORD
YOUR GOD.

DEUTERONOMY 28:2

. . . YOU ARE BLESSED, BECAUSE THE SPIRIT OF GLORY AND OF GOD RESTS UPON YOU.

1 PETER 4:14

EQUIP YOU WITH EVERYTHING
GOOD THAT YOU MAY DO
HIS WILL, WORKING IN US
THAT WHICH IS PLEASING IN
HIS SIGHT, THROUGH JESUS
CHRIST, TO WHOM BE GLORY
FOREVER AND EVER. AMEN.

HEBREWS 13:21

THE LORD BLESS YOU AND KEEP YOU . . .

NUMBERS 6:24

FOR I, THE LORD, DO NOT CHANGE . . .

MALACHI 3:6

IF ANY OF YOU
LACK WISDOM,
LET HIM ASK OF
GOD, THAT GIVETH
TO ALL MEN
LIBERALLY, AND
UPBRAIDETH NOT;
AND IT SHALL BE
GIVEN HIM.

JAMES 1:5

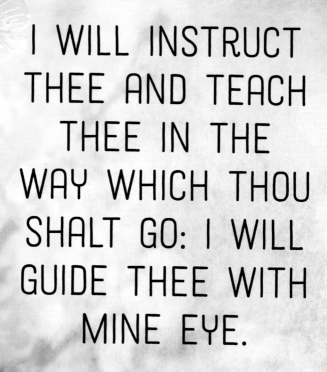

I WILL INSTRUCT THEE AND TEACH THEE IN THE WAY WHICH THOU SHALT GO: I WILL GUIDE THEE WITH MINE EYE.

PSALMS 32:8

Trust in the
Lord with all thine
heart; and lean
not unto thine own
understanding.
In all thy ways
acknowledge him,
and he shall direct
thy paths.

PROVERBS 3:5–6

THE GRASS WITHERS, AND THE FLOWER FALLS, BUT THE WORD OF THE LORD ENDURES FOREVER.

1 PETER 1:24–25

HE ANSWERED,
"TO YOU IT HAS
BEEN GIVEN
TO KNOW THE
SECRETS OF
THE KINGDOM
OF HEAVEN . . ."

MATTHEW 13:11

AND THINE EARS SHALL HEAR A WORD BEHIND THEE, SAYING, "THIS IS THE WAY, WALK YE IN IT, WHEN YE TURN TO THE RIGHT HAND, AND WHEN YE TURN TO THE LEFT."

ISAIAH 30:21

SO SPEAK
AND SO ACT
AS THOSE
WHO ARE TO
BE JUDGED
BY THE LAW
OF LIBERTY.

JAMES 2:12

KNOW WELL THE CONDITION OF YOUR FLOCKS, AND GIVE ATTENTION TO YOUR HERDS; FOR RICHES DO NOT LAST FOREVER, NOR A CROWN FOR ALL GENERATIONS.

PROVERBS 27:23–24

Wherein God, willing more abundantly to shew unto the heirs of promise the immutability of his counsel, confirmed it by an oath . . .

HEBREWS 6:17

HEAR COUNSEL, AND
RECEIVE INSTRUCTION,
THAT THOU MAYEST BE
WISE IN THY LATTER
END. THERE ARE MANY
DEVICES IN A MAN'S
HEART; NEVERTHELESS
THE COUNSEL OF THE
LORD, THAT SHALL
STAND.

PROVERBS 19:20-21

THE LORD IS MY SHEPHERD; I SHALL NOT WANT.

PSALMS 23:1

TRUST YE IN THE LORD FOR EVER: FOR IN THE LORD JEHOVAH IS EVERLASTING STRENGTH . . .

ISAIAH 26:4

THERE HATH NO
TEMPTATION TAKEN
YOU BUT SUCH AS IS
COMMON TO MAN: BUT
GOD IS FAITHFUL, WHO
WILL NOT SUFFER YOU
TO BE TEMPTED ABOVE
THAT YE ARE ABLE;
BUT WILL WITH THE
TEMPTATION ALSO MAKE
A WAY TO ESCAPE,
THAT YE MAY BE ABLE
TO BEAR IT.

1 CORINTHIANS 10:13

HE SHALL COVER
THEE WITH
HIS FEATHERS,
AND UNDER HIS
WINGS SHALT
THOU TRUST: HIS
TRUTH SHALL BE
THY SHIELD AND
BUCKLER.

PSALMS 91:4

"Honor your father and mother," which is the first commandment with a promise . . .

EPHESIANS 6:2

Therefore, do not let anyone judge you by what you eat or drink, or, with regard to a religious festival, a New Moon celebration or a Sabbath day. These are a shadow of the things that were to come; the reality, however, is found in Christ.

COLOSSIANS 2:16

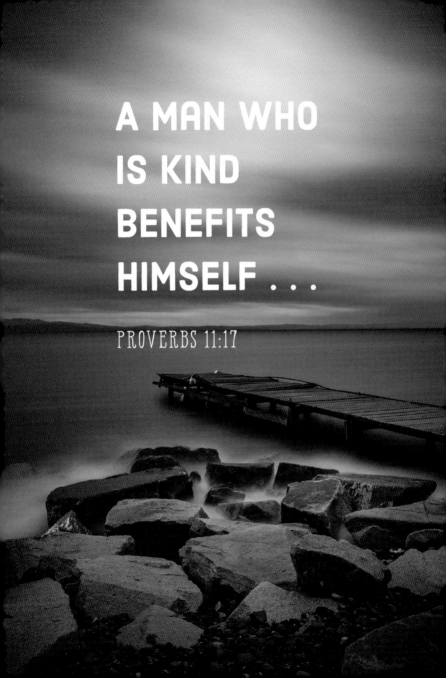

THOU SHALT NOT BE AFRAID FOR THE TERROR BY NIGHT; NOR FOR THE ARROW THAT FLIETH BY DAY; NOR FOR THE PESTILENCE THAT WALKETH IN DARKNESS; NOR FOR THE DESTRUCTION THAT WASTETH AT NOONDAY.

PSALMS 91:5-6

HE GIVETH
POWER TO THE
FAINT; AND TO
THEM THAT
HAVE NO MIGHT
HE INCREASETH
STRENGTH.

ISAIAH 40:29

He said to them, "Because of your little faith. For truly I tell you, if you have faith the size of a mustard seed, you will say to this mountain, 'Move from here to there,' and it will move; and nothing will be impossible for you."

MATTHEW 17:20

BUT THOU, O LORD, ART A SHIELD FOR ME; MY GLORY, AND THE LIFTER UP OF MINE HEAD.

PSALMS 3:3

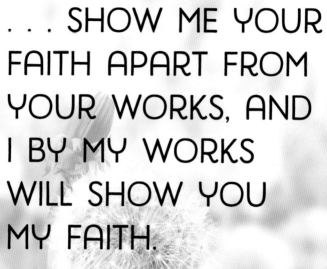

. . . SHOW ME YOUR FAITH APART FROM YOUR WORKS, AND I BY MY WORKS WILL SHOW YOU MY FAITH.

JAMES 2:18

IN GOD HAVE I
PUT MY TRUST:
I WILL NOT BE
AFRAID WHAT
MAN CAN DO
UNTO ME.

PSALMS 56:11

In whom we have boldness and access with confidence by the faith of him.

EPHESIANS 3:12

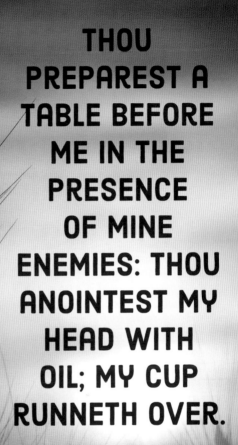

THOU PREPAREST A TABLE BEFORE ME IN THE PRESENCE OF MINE ENEMIES: THOU ANOINTEST MY HEAD WITH OIL; MY CUP RUNNETH OVER.

PSALMS 23:5

YET IF THERE IS AN ANGEL AT THEIR SIDE, A MESSENGER, ONE OUT OF A THOUSAND, SENT TO TELL THEM HOW TO BE UPRIGHT . . .

JOB 33:23

HE REFRESHES MY SOUL. HE GUIDES ME ALONG THE RIGHT PATHS FOR HIS NAME'S SAKE.

PSALMS 23:3

THE MOUTHS
OF THE
RIGHTEOUS
UTTER
WISDOM,
AND THEIR
TONGUES
SPEAK WHAT
IS JUST.

PSALMS 37:30

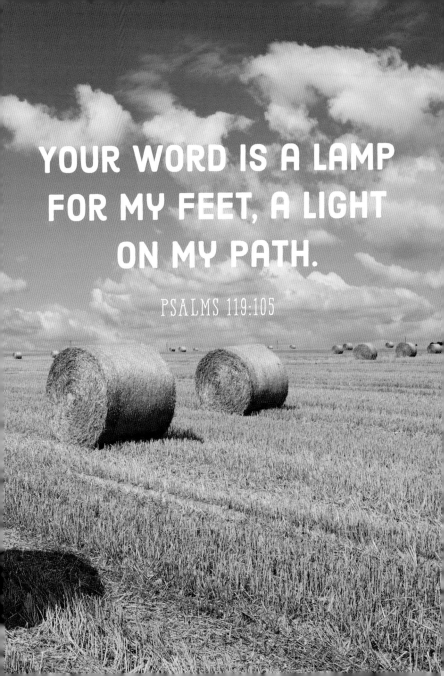

But when he, the Spirit of truth, comes, he will guide you into all the truth. He will not speak on his own; he will speak only what he hears, and he will tell you what is yet to come.

JOHN 16:13

GOD IS OUR REFUGE AND STRENGTH, AN EVER-PRESENT HELP IN TROUBLE.

PSALMS 46:1

THE HEART
OF MAN
PLANS HIS
WAY, BUT
THE LORD
ESTABLISHES
HIS STEPS.

PROVERBS 16:9

LIKEWISE THE SPIRIT HELPS US IN OUR WEAKNESS.

ROMANS 8:26

FOR WITH YOU IS THE FOUNTAIN OF LIFE; IN YOUR LIGHT DO WE SEE LIGHT.

PSALMS 36:9

*Light is
sown for the
righteous,
and joy for
the upright
in heart.*

PSALMS 97:11

HE MAKES ME LIE DOWN IN GREEN PASTURES. HE LEADS ME BESIDE STILL WATERS.

PSALMS 23:2

TAKE MY YOKE
UPON YOU, AND
LEARN FROM ME,
FOR I AM GENTLE
AND LOWLY IN
HEART, AND YOU
WILL FIND REST
FOR YOUR SOULS.

MATTHEW 11:29

GOOD SENSE IS
A FOUNTAIN OF
LIFE TO HIM
WHO HAS IT . . .

PROVERBS 16:22

FOR THE EYES OF THE
LORD RUN TO AND
FRO THROUGHOUT THE
WHOLE EARTH, TO GIVE
STRONG SUPPORT TO
THOSE WHOSE HEART IS
BLAMELESS TOWARD HIM.

2 CHRONICLES 16:9

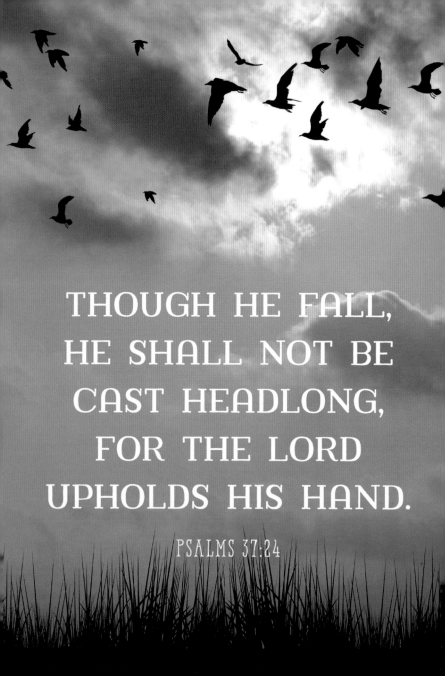

HE TRAINS MY HANDS FOR WAR, SO THAT MY ARMS CAN BEND A BOW OF BRONZE.

2 SAMUEL 22:35

THAT THIS IS
GOD, OUR GOD
FOREVER AND
EVER. HE WILL
BE OUR GUIDE
FOREVER.

PSALMS 48:14

Marvel not at this: for the hour is coming, in the which all that are in the graves shall hear his voice, and shall come forth; they that have done good, unto the resurrection of life . . .

JOHN 5:28–29

AND I AM SURE OF THIS, THAT HE WHO BEGAN A GOOD WORK IN YOU WILL BRING IT TO COMPLETION AT THE DAY OF JESUS CHRIST.

PHILIPPIANS 1:6

THAT WHOSOEVER BELIEVETH IN HIM SHOULD NOT PERISH, BUT HAVE ETERNAL LIFE.

JOHN 3:15

From now on there is reserved for me the crown of righteousness, which the Lord, the righteous judge, will give me on that day, and not only to me but also to all who have longed for his appearing.

2 TIMOTHY 4:8

IN HOPE OF ETERNAL
LIFE, WHICH GOD,
THAT CANNOT LIE,
PROMISED BEFORE
THE WORLD BEGAN . . .

TITUS 1:2

BUT TO DO GOOD AND TO COMMUNICATE FORGET NOT: FOR WITH SUCH SACRIFICES, GOD IS WELL PLEASED.

HEBREWS 13:16

NEVERTHELESS,
WE, ACCORDING
TO HIS PROMISE,
LOOK FOR NEW
HEAVENS AND
A NEW EARTH,
WHEREIN
DWELLETH
RIGHTEOUSNESS.

2 PETER 3:13

THOU SHALT
COME TO
THY GRAVE
IN A FULL
AGE, LIKE
AS A SHOCK
OF CORN
COMETH IN
HIS SEASON.

JOB 5:26

FOR THIS REASON,
CHRIST IS THE MEDIATOR
OF A NEW COVENANT,
THAT THOSE WHO ARE
CALLED MAY RECEIVE
THE PROMISED ETERNAL
INHERITANCE . . . .

HEBREWS 9:15

THEY WILL SEE HIS FACE, AND HIS NAME WILL BE ON THEIR FOREHEADS.

REVELATION 22:4

And the world and its desire are passing away, but those who do the will of God live forever.

1 JOHN 2:17

. . . there is now no condemnation for those who are in Christ Jesus because through Christ Jesus the Law of the Spirit who gives life has set you free . . .

ROMANS 8:1–2

HUMBLE YOURSELVES, THEREFORE, UNDER THE MIGHTY HAND OF GOD SO THAT AT THE PROPER TIME HE MAY EXALT YOU . . .

1 PETER 5:6

NOTWITHSTANDING IN THIS REJOICE NOT, THAT THE SPIRITS ARE SUBJECT UNTO YOU; BUT RATHER REJOICE, BECAUSE YOUR NAMES ARE WRITTEN IN HEAVEN.

LUKE 10:20

Those that be planted in the house of the Lord shall flourish in the courts of our God.

PSALMS 92:13

LO, CHILDREN ARE A HERITAGE FROM THE LORD: AND THE FRUIT OF THE WOMB IS HIS REWARD. AS ARROWS ARE IN THE HAND OF A MIGHT MAN; SO ARE THE CHILDREN OF THE YOUTH.

PSALMS 127:3-4

THOSE THE LORD
HAS RESCUED
WILL RETURN.
THEY WILL
ENTER ZION
WITH SINGING;
EVERLASTING
JOY WILL CROWN
THEIR HEADS . . .

ISAIAH 51:11

TO THE ONE WHO
CONQUERS I WILL GIVE
A PLACE WITH ME ON
MY THRONE, JUST AS
I MYSELF CONQUERED
AND SAT DOWN WITH MY
FATHER ON HIS THRONE.

REVELATIONS 3:21

TO THOSE WHO
BY PATIENTLY
DOING GOOD
SEEK FOR GLORY
AND HONOR AND
IMMORTALITY,
HE WILL GIVE
ETERNAL LIFE . . .

ROMANS 2:7

But, as it is written,
"What no eye has
seen, nor ear heard,
nor the human heart
conceived, what God
has prepared for those
who love him . . ."

CORINTHIANS 2:9

IN MY FATHER'S HOUSE ARE
MANY MANSIONS: IF IT WERE
NOT SO, I WOULD HAVE TOLD
YOU. I GO TO PREPARE A PLACE
FOR YOU. AND IF I GO AND
PREPARE A PLACE FOR YOU, I
WILL COME AGAIN, AND RECEIVE
YOU UNTO MYSELF; THAT WHERE
I AM, THERE YE MAY BE ALSO.

JOHN 14:2-3

LET ANYONE WHO
HAS AN EAR LISTEN
TO WHAT THE
SPIRIT IS SAYING
TO THE CHURCHES.
TO EVERYONE WHO
CONQUERS, I WILL GIVE
PERMISSION TO EAT
FROM THE TREE OF
LIFE THAT IS IN THE
PARADISE OF GOD.

REVELATION 2:7

For the Lord himself shall descend from heaven with a shout, with the voice of the archangel, and with the trump of God: and the dead in Christ shall rise first . . .

1 THESSALONIANS 4:16

AND WHEN
THE CHIEF
SHEPHERD
APPEARS,
YOU WILL
RECEIVE THE
UNFADING
CROWN OF
GLORY.

1 PETER 5:3-4

THEN THE
RIGHTEOUS WILL
SHINE LIKE THE
SUN IN THE
KINGDOM OF
THEIR FATHER. HE
WHO HAS EARS,
LET HIM HEAR.

MATTHEW 13:43

THEN WE WHICH ARE ALIVE AND REMAIN SHALL BE CAUGHT UP TOGETHER WITH THEM IN THE CLOUDS, TO MEET THE LORD IN THE AIR: AND SO SHALL WE EVER BE WITH THE LORD.

1 THESSALONIANS 4:17

AND GOD SHALL WIPE
AWAY ALL TEARS FROM
THEIR EYES; AND THERE
SHALL BE NO MORE DEATH,
NEITHER SORROW, NOR
CRYING, NEITHER SHALL
THERE BE ANY MORE PAIN:
FOR THE FORMER THINGS
ARE PASSED AWAY.

REVELATION 21:4

PRECIOUS TREASURE AND OIL ARE IN A WISE MAN'S DWELLING, BUT A FOOLISH MAN DEVOURS IT.

PROVERBS 21:20

And we receive from him whatever we ask, because we obey his commandments and do what pleases him.

1 JOHN 3:22

GRAY HAIR IS A CROWN OF GLORY; IT IS GAINED IN A RIGHTEOUS LIFE.

PROVERBS 16:31

Take delight
in the Lord,
and he will
give you the
desires of
your heart.

PSALMS 37:4

BY THIS WE
KNOW THAT
WE ABIDE
IN HIM AND
HE IN US,
BECAUSE HE
HAS GIVEN US
OF HIS SPIRIT.

1 JOHN 4:13

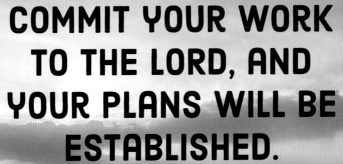

COMMIT YOUR WORK
TO THE LORD, AND
YOUR PLANS WILL BE
ESTABLISHED.

PROVERBS 16:3

. . . HE REWARDS
THOSE WHO SEEK HIM.

HEBREWS 11:6

THE RIGHTEOUSNESS OF THE UPRIGHT DELIVERS THEM . . .

PROVERBS 11:6

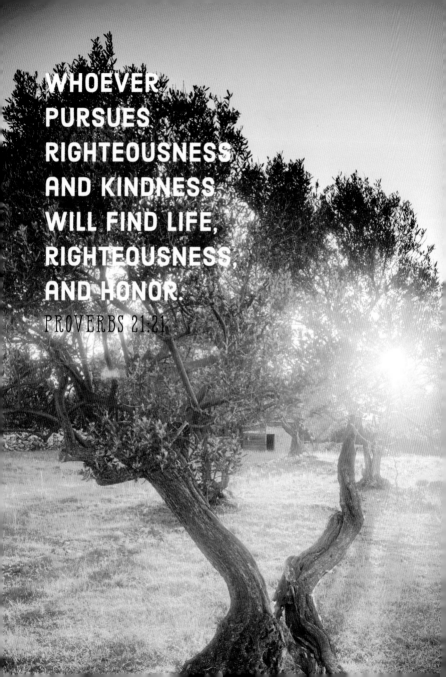

I WILL MAKE AN EVERLASTING COVENANT WITH THEM, NEVER TO DRAW BACK FROM DOING GOOD TO THEM . . .

JEREMIAH 32:40

. . . PRAY
TO YOUR
FATHER
WHO IS IN
SECRET;
AND YOUR
FATHER
WHO SEES
IN SECRET
WILL
REWARD
YOU.

MATTHEW 6:6

FOR ALL THE PROMISES OF GOD IN HIM ARE YEA, AND IN HIM AMEN, UNTO THE GLORY OF GOD BY US.

2 CORINTHIANS 1:20

He will glorify
me because it
is from me that
he will receive
what he will
make known
to you.

JOHN 16:14

BE WISE, MY
CHILD, AND
MAKE MY HEART
GLAD, SO THAT
I MAY ANSWER
WHOEVER
REPROACHES ME.

PROVERBS 27:11

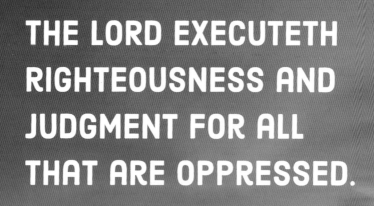

THE LORD EXECUTETH RIGHTEOUSNESS AND JUDGMENT FOR ALL THAT ARE OPPRESSED.

PSALMS 103:6

Your throne,
O God, endures
forever and
ever. Your
royal scepter
is a scepter
of equity . . .

PSALMS 45:6

CALL UNTO ME,
AND I WILL
ANSWER THEE,
AND SHOW THEE
GREAT AND
MIGHTY THINGS,
WHICH THOU
KNOWEST NOT.

JEREMIAH 33:3

For those God foreknew, he also predestined to be conformed to the image of his Son, that he might be the firstborn among many brothers and sisters.

ROMANS 8:29

HE DETERMINES THE NUMBER OF THE STARS; HE GIVES TO ALL OF THEM THEIR NAMES.

PSALMS 147:4

I make known the end from the beginning, from ancient times, what is still to come.

ISAIAH 46:10

THE FRIENDSHIP OF THE LORD IS FOR THOSE WHO FEAR HIM, AND HE MAKES HIS COVENANT KNOWN TO THEM.

PSALMS 25:14

KNOW, THEREFORE, THAT THE LORD YOUR GOD IS GOD, THE FAITHFUL GOD WHO MAINTAINS COVENANT LOYALTY WITH THOSE WHO LOVE HIM AND KEEP HIS COMMANDMENTS, TO A THOUSAND GENERATIONS . . .

DEUTERONOMY 7:9

WHO CONFIRMS
THE WORD OF HIS
SERVANT, AND
FULFILLS THE
PREDICTION OF HIS
MESSENGERS . . .

ISAIAH 44:26

AND THE
WORDS OF
THE LORD ARE
FLAWLESS,
LIKE SILVER
PURIFIED IN A
CRUCIBLE, LIKE
GOLD REFINED
SEVEN TIMES.

PSALMS 12:6

The Lord is not slow in keeping his promise, as some understand slowness. Instead he is patient with you, not wanting anyone to perish, but everyone to come to repentance.

2 PETER 3:9

JESUS WENT ON TO SAY, "IN A LITTLE WHILE YOU WILL SEE ME NO MORE, AND THEN AFTER A LITTLE WHILE YOU WILL SEE ME."

JOHN 16:16

... HIS APPEARING IS AS SURE AS THE DAWN; HE WILL COME TO US LIKE THE SHOWERS, LIKE THE SPRING RAINS THAT WATER THE EARTH.

HOSEA 6:3

Yet you, Lord, are our Father. We are the clay, you are the potter; we are all the work of your hand.

ISAIAH 64:8

EVERY GOOD AND
PERFECT GIFT IS FROM
ABOVE, COMING DOWN
FROM THE FATHER OF
THE HEAVENLY LIGHTS,
WHO DOES NOT
CHANGE LIKE SHIFTING
SHADOWS.

JAMES 1:17

I REMAIN CONFIDENT OF THIS: I WILL SEE THE GOODNESS OF THE LORD IN THE LAND OF THE LIVING.

PSALMS 27:13

THE SPIRIT OF GOD HAS MADE ME; THE BREATH OF THE ALMIGHTY GIVES ME LIFE.

JOB 33:4

The unfolding
of your words
gives light;
it imparts
understanding
to the simple.

PSALMS 119:130

FOR SURELY I KNOW THE PLANS I HAVE FOR YOU, SAYS THE LORD, PLANS FOR YOUR WELFARE AND NOT FOR HARM, TO GIVE YOU A FUTURE WITH HOPE.

JEREMIAH 29:11

BEFORE I FORMED
YOU IN THE WOMB I
KNEW YOU . . .

JEREMIAH 1:5

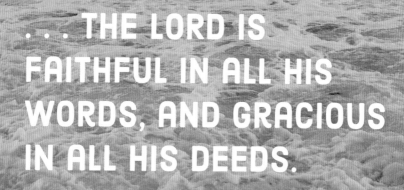

. . . THE LORD IS FAITHFUL IN ALL HIS WORDS, AND GRACIOUS IN ALL HIS DEEDS.

PSALMS 145:13

GRACIOUS IS THE LORD, AND RIGHTEOUS; OUR GOD IS MERCIFUL.

PSALMS 116:5

For he does
not willingly
afflict or
grieve anyone.

LAMENTATIONS 3:33

BUT YOU ARE A CHOSEN
RACE, A ROYAL PRIESTHOOD,
A HOLY NATION, A PEOPLE
FOR HIS OWN POSSESSION,
THAT YOU MAY PROCLAIM THE
EXCELLENCIES OF HIM WHO
CALLED YOU OUT OF DARKNESS
INTO HIS MARVELOUS LIGHT.

1 PETER 2:9

"YOU ARE MY WITNESSES," DECLARES THE LORD, "AND MY SERVANT WHOM I HAVE CHOSEN . . ."

ISAIAH 43:10

May grace and peace be multiplied to you in the knowledge of God and of Jesus our Lord.

2 PETER 1:2

FOR THE
WORD OF
THE LORD
IS RIGHT;
AND ALL
HIS WORKS
ARE DONE
IN TRUTH.

PSALMS 33:4

GOD IS NOT A MAN, THAT HE SHOULD LIE; NEITHER THE SON OF MAN, THAT HE SHOULD REPENT: HATH HE SAID, AND SHALL HE NOT DO IT? OR HATH HE SPOKEN, AND SHALL HE NOT MAKE IT GOOD?

NUMBERS 23:19

FOR GOD IS THE KING
OF ALL THE EARTH:
SING YE PRAISES WITH
UNDERSTANDING. GOD
REIGNETH OVER THE
HEATHEN: GOD SITTETH
UPON THE THRONE OF
HIS HOLINESS.

PSALMS 47:7-8

AS IN THE DAYS
WHEN YOU CAME
OUT OF EGYPT, I
WILL SHOW THEM
MY WONDERS.

MICAH 7:15

He chose to give us
birth through the
word of truth, that
we might be a kind
of firstfruits of all
he created.

JAMES 1:18

HE HIMSELF BORE OUR SINS IN HIS BODY ON THE CROSS, SO THAT WE MIGHT DIE TO SINS AND LIVE FOR RIGHTEOUSNESS; BY HIS WOUNDS YOU HAVE BEEN HEALED.

1 PETER 2:24

THUS HE HAS GIVEN US, THROUGH THESE THINGS, HIS PRECIOUS AND VERY GREAT PROMISES, SO THAT THROUGH THEM YOU MAY . . . BECOME PARTICIPANTS OF THE DIVINE NATURE.

2 PETER 1:4

He shatters
the doors of
bronze, and
cuts in two the
bars of iron.

PSALMS 107:16

Every way of a man
is right in his own
eyes, but the Lord
weighs the heart.

PROVERBS 21:2

FOR THE PROMISE IS
FOR YOU, FOR YOUR
CHILDREN, AND FOR
ALL WHO ARE FAR
AWAY, EVERYONE
WHOM THE LORD OUR
GOD CALLS TO HIM.

ACTS 2:39

THE FATHER LOVES
THE SON AND HAS
PLACED ALL THINGS
IN HIS HANDS.

JOHN 3:35

And because you are children, God has sent the spirit of his son into our hearts . . .

GALATIANS 4:6

THERE IS
NO LONGER SLAVE OR
FREE, THERE IS NO
LONGER MALE AND
FEMALE; FOR ALL
OF YOU ARE ONE IN
CHRIST JESUS.

GALATIANS 3:28

HE WHOM GOD HAS SENT SPEAKS THE WORDS OF GOD, FOR HE GIVES THE SPIRIT WITHOUT MEASURE.

JOHN 3:34

THE MOUNTAINS MELT
LIKE WAX BEFORE THE
LORD, BEFORE THE LORD
OF ALL THE EARTH.

PSALMS 97:5

FROM AGES PAST
NO ONE HAS
HEARD, NO EAR
HAS PERCEIVED,
NO EYE HAS SEEN
ANY GOD BESIDES
YOU, WHO WORKS
FOR THOSE WHO
WAIT FOR HIM.

ISAIAH 64:4

HE IS THE SOURCE OF
YOUR LIFE IN CHRIST
JESUS, WHO BECAME FOR
US WISDOM FROM GOD,
AND RIGHTEOUSNESS AND
SANCTIFICATION AND
REDEMPTION,

1 CORINTHIANS 1:29–30

THE LORD EXISTS FOREVER;
YOUR WORD IS FIRMLY
FIXED IN HEAVEN.

PSALMS 119:89

O SAVE YOUR PEOPLE,
AND BLESS YOUR
HERITAGE; BE THEIR
SHEPHERD, AND CARRY
THEM FOREVER.

PSALMS 28:9

THE COUNSEL OF
THE LORD STANDS
FOREVER, THE
THOUGHTS OF
HIS HEART TO ALL
GENERATIONS.

PSALMS 33:11